First published in the United States in 1999 by Peter Bedrick Books
A division of NTC/Contemporary Publishing Group, Inc
4255 West Touhy Avenue
Lincolnwood (Chicago), Illinois 60646-1975 U.S.A.

Editor: Lisa Edwards
Designer: Kate Buxton
Language consultant: Ann Lazim,
Centre for Language in Primary Education
Natural History consultant: Brian Bett,
Southampton Oceanography Centre

Library of Congress Cataloging-in-Publication Data
Baker, Alan.
    The ocean / Alan Baker. – 1st American ed.
        p.   cm. –   (Look who lives in--)
    Summary: A simple introduction to the variety of animals living in
the ocean, including the seahorse, octopus, and swordfish.
    ISBN 0-87226-539-0 (hardcover)
    1.   Marine animals--Juvenile literature.   [1. Marine animals.]
I. Title. II Title: Look who lives in the ocean. III. Series:
Baker, Alan, 1951-   Look who lives in--
QL 122.2.B35   1999
591.77--DC21   98-37549
                                                                   CIP
                                                                    AC

Printed and bound in Portugal by Edições ASA

International Standard Book Number: 0-87226-539-0

99   00   01   02   03   15   14   13   12   11   10   9   8   7   6   5   4   3   2   1

LOOK WHO LIVES IN...

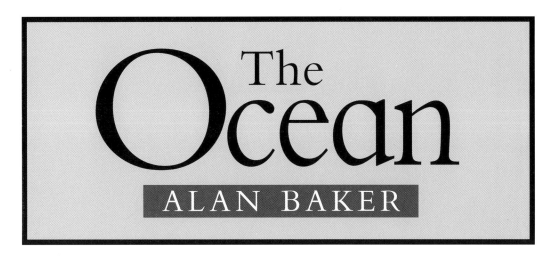

The Ocean

ALAN BAKER

PETER BEDRICK BOOKS

NEW YORK

Deep down near the ocean
floor, something is looking
at a crab.
It's a dainty, delicate. . .

seahorse!
It has a long snout and a coiled tail.
Gliding among the rocks and weeds,
something is looking at the seahorse.
It's a slippery, slithering. . .

eel!
With its long, thin body it looks
a bit like a snake.
Swimming in the deep, dark waters,
something is looking at the eel.
It's a wriggling, writhing. . .

octopus!
It has eight very long arms.
Peering through the murky gloom,
something is looking at the octopus.
It's a smooth, sleek. . .

ray!
It's got a very flat body and a long,
whip-like tail.
Swimming in the clear, blue waters,
something is looking at the ray.
It's a diving, darting. . .

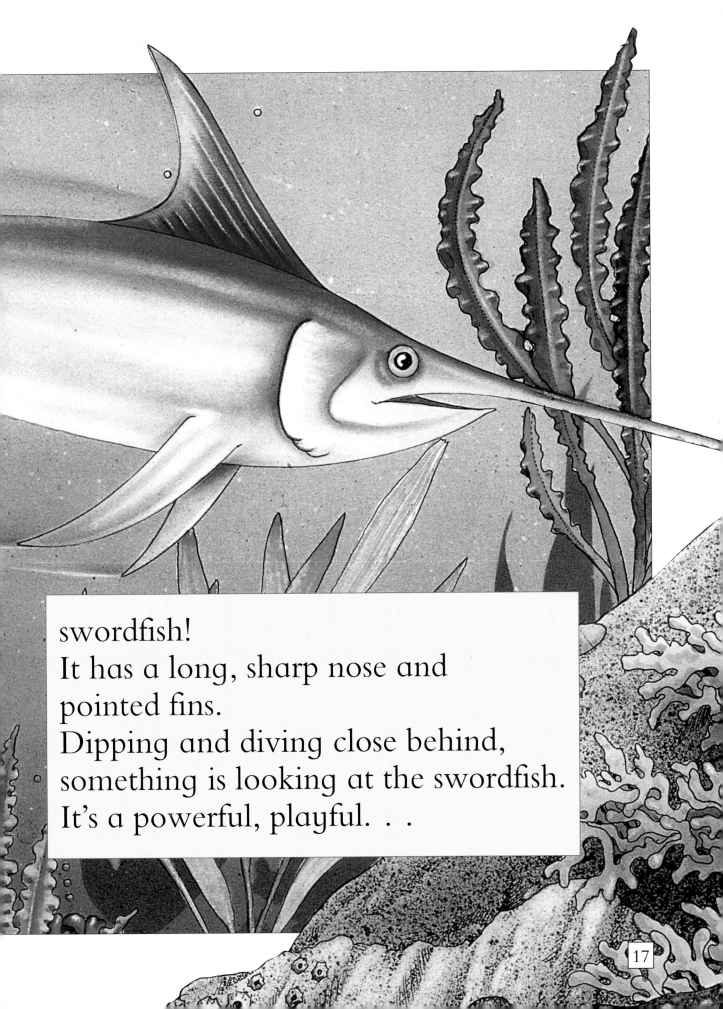

swordfish!
It has a long, sharp nose and
pointed fins.
Dipping and diving close behind,
something is looking at the swordfish.
It's a powerful, playful. . .

dolphin!
It has a beautiful, smooth, blue
and white body.
With tiny eyes, something with very
sharp teeth is looking at the dolphin.
It's a deadly, dangerous. . .

shark!
It's got skin like sandpaper,
made of tough, tiny scales.
Swimming in the sunlit waters,
something is looking at the shark.
It's a soaring, swooping. . .

flying fish!
They have fins just like wings.
Swimming calmly near the surface
of the water, something is looking
at the flying fish.
It's a sleepy, scaly. . .

turtle!
This one is two hundred years old.
With an enormous mouth and
gentle eyes, something is looking
at the turtle.
It's a massive, magnificent. . .

blue whale!
It's the largest animal
in the world. It's looking at all
the animals – the turtle, the flying
fish, the shark, the dolphin, the
swordfish, the ray, the octopus,
the eel, the seahorse and the crab.
Can *you* see them all?

The World's Oceans

About two-thirds of the earth is covered by salty sea water. 'Ocean' is the term we give to large areas of sea water. You can see the world's five major oceans on the map below. They are home to a huge variety of animals and plants. The biggest ocean is the Pacific. It is almost as large as all the other oceans put together.

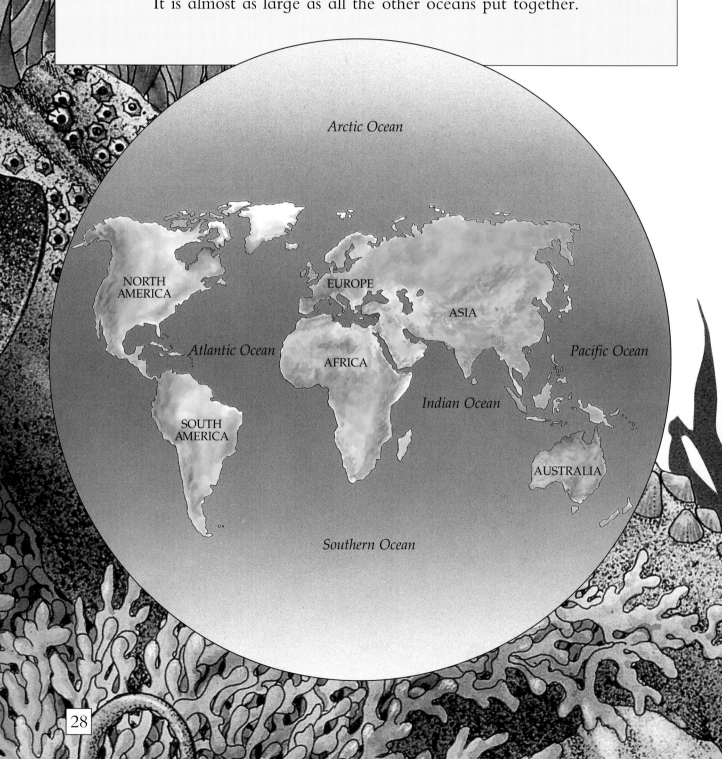

Arctic Ocean

NORTH AMERICA

EUROPE

ASIA

Atlantic Ocean

AFRICA

Pacific Ocean

Indian Ocean

SOUTH AMERICA

AUSTRALIA

Southern Ocean

PAGE 7: Crabs have their skeleton on the outside of their bodies. It is a hard shell that helps to protect them from predators. They also have a pair of sharp pincers.

PAGE 8: Seahorses are covered in a kind of body armor made of bony rings. The male has a pocket beneath its tail in which the female lays her eggs.

PAGE 10: Conger eels hide among plants and rocks on the sea floor. At night, they come out to hunt fish. They can grow up to 9 feet long.

PAGE 12: Octopuses can change color to blend in with their surroundings. They can spurt out a black liquid which acts as a screen to help them escape from predators.

PAGE 15: Stingrays often lie partly buried on the sea floor. They have very poisonous spines on their tails. A small amount of poison can make a person unconscious.

PAGE 17: Swordfish have flat 'swords' that extend from their snouts. They use them to slash at their prey. Sometimes, their broken swords can be found in the hulls of ships.

PAGE 19: Dolphins are the smallest of all the whales. They live in groups of up to 100. Dolphins are the most playful and intelligent of all sea creatures.

PAGE 20: Sharks have sharp teeth, which they use to tear at their prey. They can get so excited while they are feeding that they eat other sharks.

PAGE 22: Flying fish have either two or four wings and they grow to about 17 inches in length. They can throw themselves into the air and glide for up to forty seconds.

PAGE 24: Turtles lay their eggs in sand. Once a year, females bury about 100 eggs, away from the water's edge. When baby turtles hatch, they scramble to the water.

PAGE 27: Blue whales are the biggest animals in the world. They can grow up to 96 feet long and weigh nearly 150 tons. They breathe through a blowhole.

Most of the plants in the ocean are types of algae (pronounced 'algay'). They mostly live in the top 480 feet of the sea where it is sunny. The tiniest plants, called plankton, drift near the surface. The biggest algae are sea-weeds which are attached to the sea bed.